Thomas M. Meine

THE AUBURNDALE
WATCH COMPANY
First American Attempt
toward the Dollar Watch

Contributions from the Museum of History and Technology, United States National Museum, Smithsonian Institution, Washington D.C., Bulletin 218, paper 4, page 49 – 68, 1959, **by Edwin A. Battison**

Bibliographic information published by the Deutsche
Nationalbibliothek:

The Deutsche Nationalbibliothek lists this publication in the
Deutsche Nationalbibliografie; detailed bibliographic data
are available on the Internet at http://dnb.dnb.de

Herstellung und Verlag: BoD – Books
on Demand, Norderstedt

December 2021

ISBN 9 783755 753742

CONTENT

Note: Some spelling/punctuation mistakes or printing errors in the original work have been corrected, which means minor and insignificant changes from the original text. Other possible issues were mostly left unchanged.

Endnotes have been left at the end of the book, as they mostly are too large to be directly inserted into the text or shown as footnotes at the individual pages.

Efforts have been made to improve images and drawings available from the original source. This was, however, only possible to a limited extent; the reader is therefore kindly asked to accept an occasional lower printing quality. The overall layout has been optimized for a print book and the e-book version.

By Edwin A. Battison

THE AUBURNDALE WATCH COMPANY
First American Attempt toward the Dollar Watch

INTRODUCTION

The life of the pioneer has always been arduous. Not all succeeded, and many disappeared, leaving no trace on the pages of history. Here, a painstaking search has uncovered enough of the record to permit us to review the errors of design and manufacture that brought failure to the first attempt to produce a really cheap pocket watch.

This paper is based on a study of the patent model of the Auburndale rotary and other products of the company in the collections of the National Museum, and of other collections, including that of the author. The study comprises part of the background research for the hall of timekeeping in the Museum of History and Technology.

The Author: *Edwin A. Battison is associate curator of mechanical and civil engineering, Museum of History and Technology, at the Smithsonian Institution's United States National Museum.*

The idea of a machine-made watch with interchangeable parts had been in the minds of many men for a long time. Several attempts had been made to translate this conception into a reality. Success crowned the efforts of those working near Boston, Massachusetts, in the 1850s. The work done there formed the basis on which American watch making grew to such a point that by the 1870s watches of domestic manufacture had captured nearly all the home market and were reaching out and capturing foreign markets as well. In spite of this great achievement, there remained a large untapped potential market for a watch which would combine the virtues of close time keeping and a lower selling price. Only a radical departure in design could achieve this. Rivalry between the several existing companies had already produced an irreducible minimum price on watches of conventional design.

The great obstacle to close rate in a modestly priced watch is the balance wheel. This wheel requires careful adjustment for temperature error and for poise. Of these two disturbing factors, poise is the most annoying to the owner because lack of it makes the watch a very erratic timekeeper. A watch in which the parts are not poised is subject to a different rate for every position it is placed in. This position error, as it is called, can and often does cause a most erratic and unpredictable rate. Abraham-Louis Breguet, the celebrated Swiss-French horologist of Paris, is credited with the invention, in 1801 **[endnote 1]**, of his tourbillon, a clever way to circumvent this error.

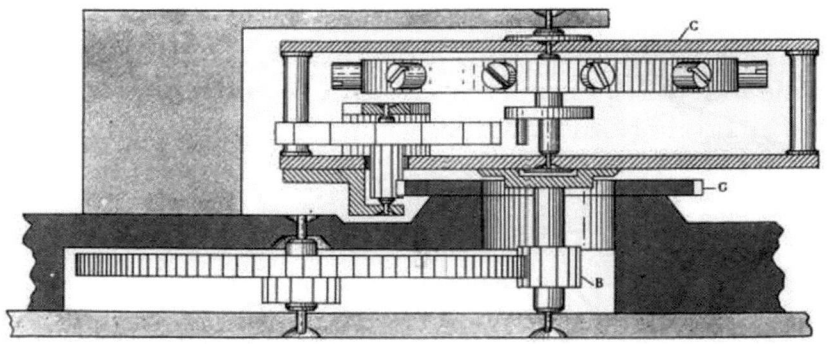

Figure 1 – Breguet'S Tourbillon. At C is shown the carriage which revolves with pinion B carrying the escapement and balance around the stationary wheel G. (After G. A. Baillie, *Watches, their history, decoration, and mechanism*, London, Methuen, n.d.)

His solution was to mount the escapement in a frame or 'chariot' which revolved, usually once a minute, so that with each revolution all possible positions were passed through **(Figure 1)**. This gave the watch an average rate which was constant except for variations within the period of revolution of the chariot. Only a very skillful workman could, however, work with the delicacy necessary to produce such a mechanism. The result was that few were made, and these were so expensive that it continued to be more practical to poise the parts in a conventional movement. The idea of revolving the entire train of a watch, including the escapement, seems to have evolved surprisingly slowly from Breguet's basic invention of the revolving escapement. In constructing a watch wherein the entire train revolves, no such delicate or precise workmanship is required as in the tourbillon. Due to the longer train of gears involved, the period of revolution is much slower. Position errors average out as certainly, if not as frequently. In Bonniksen's 'Karrusel' watch of 1893 **[endnote 2]** the duration of a cycle is 52.5 minutes **[endnote 3]** while in the Auburndale Rotary, which we are about to discuss, the period of each revolution is 2 1/2 hours.

THE INVENTION

The patent model of Jason R. Hopkins' revolving watch, now in the U. S. National Museum **[endnote 4]**, was not the first in which the entire train revolved, but it was a very novel conception intended to reduce greatly the number of parts usually associated with any watch. This may be seen from **Figures 2 and 3**, where everything shown inside the ring gear revolves slowly as the main spring runs down. This spring is prevented from running down at its own speed by the train pinion seen in mesh with the ring gear. Through this, pinion motion is imparted to the escape wheel and balance, where the rate of the watch is controlled. The balance, being planted at the center of revolution, travels around its own axis, as in the tourbillon, at the speed with which the entire train revolves around the barrel arbor. This arbor turns only during winding. No dial or dial gearing is shown in the patent or exists in the patent model. The patent merely says, casually, 'By means of dial wheels the motion of the barrel may be communicated to hands and the time indicated in the usual manner.' No fine finish or jeweling has been lavished on the model; the only jewels present being in the balance cock which was utilized as it came from its original watch, with only minor modifications to the shape of its foot. Apparently, the balance wheel itself is also a relic of the same or a similar conventional watch. There is no jeweling in the escapement or on the other end of the balance staff. In spite of this, the model runs very actively and will overbank if wound up very far. The beat of the escapement is two per second and the movement revolves once in 20 minutes.

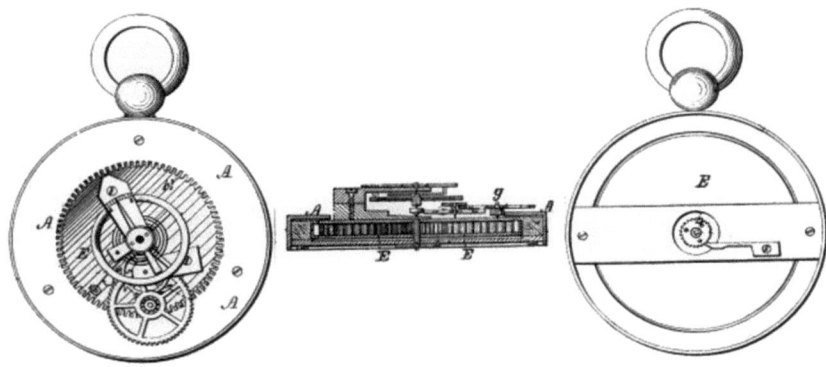

Figure 2 – Patent Drawing of the Hopkins Watch. The mainspring barrel *E*, of a very large diameter in proportion to the diameter of the watch, occupies nearly the full diameter of the movement. The spring itself, narrower and much longer than usual, is made in the patent model by riveting two ordinary springs together end to end. Over this barrel and attached to the stationary frame of the watch is placed a large thin ring A, cut on its inner diameter with 120 teeth. Near its edge the barrel E carries a stud *g* on which runs a pinion of 10 in mesh with the ring gear *A*. On this pinion is a wheel of 80 driving a pinion of 6 on the escape-wheel arbor. The 15-tooth escape wheel locks on a spring detent and gives impulse to the balance in one direction only, being a conventional chronometer escapement. The intermediate wheel and pinion, balance wheel, and balance cock have been adapted from a Swiss bar movement of the time.

Figure 3 – Original Patent Model of the Hopkins Watch, U. S. Patent 161513, July 20, 1875, now in the U. S. National Museum (*cat. no.* 309025).

There are two great faults in the model. First is the lack of an adequate bearing for the barrel to turn on. There is only one very short bearing a long way removed from the point of engagement between the pinion and internal gear, and no adequate support is given to the barrel, with the result that it tends to deflect from the ideal or true position and to bind. This condition is aggravated by the fact that the ring gear was made by cutting its teeth on an angle to the axis around which it is to revolve, using only a saw of appropriate width. The teeth were then rounded-up to form by hand in a separate operation, which by its very nature means that the teeth are not exactly alike. This lack of uniformity of the ring gear coupled with an entirely inadequate bearing for the barrel contributes to rather erratic transfer of power. These irregular teeth would not, of course, be a factor in factory-made watches where suitable machinery would be available for the work.

The second fault is in the ratio between the time of one revolution and the number of revolutions necessary for a day's run. Three turns of the spring are, of course, required to run the watch for an hour, since the barrel and train revolve three times in that length of time. If we choose to have the watch run for 30 hours on a winding, and this leaves but a small safety factor, then we see that this will require 90 turns of the main spring, a manifest impossibility in view of the space available **[endnote 5]**.

Probably no attempt was made to produce a finished and practical watch at this time, although Hopkins, the inventor, was an actual watchmaker as well as a retail jeweler, with premises virtually in the shadow of the Patent Office. He was a native of Maine **[endnote 6]** and had been established in Washington since 1863, or perhaps some time in 1862 **[endnote 7]**.

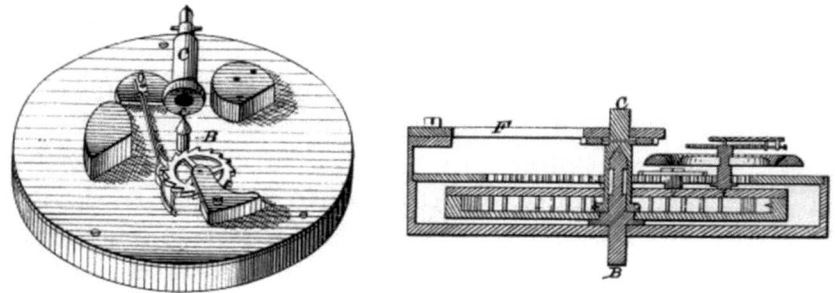

Figure 4 – Drawing from U. S. Patent 165831, showing Hopkins' first design improvement, an arbor for the barrel and train to turn on and the balance displaced from center.

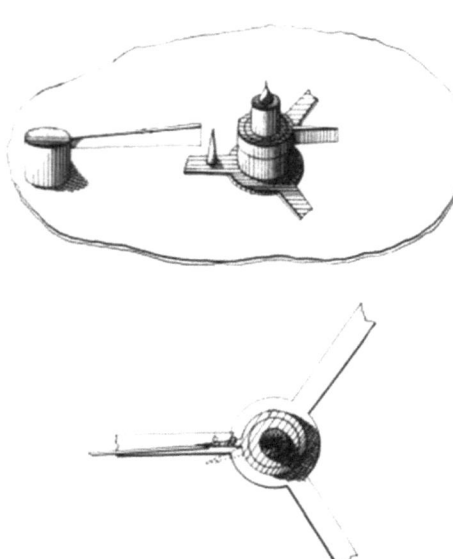

Figure 5 (left) – Hopkins' Balance Arresting Device, the subject of U. S. patent 165830.

This and the device illustrated in **Figure 4 (above)** were originally submitted together to the Patent Office on June 9, 1875, and later were divided into two patents.

DEVELOPING THE IDEA

Edward A. Locke had long been seeking a simple watch adapted to easy manufacture and a selling price of three to four dollars. While on a trip to Washington his attention was drawn to the Hopkins watch by William D. Colt of Washington **[endnote 8]**. A result of this meeting appears to have been the issuance to Jason R. Hopkins of two patents, **[endnote 9]** in both of which half rights were assigned to William D. Colt. Patent 165831, relates to a barrel arbor for watches. The arbor will be seen **(Figure 4)** to consist of two parts, one telescoped within the other, and the composite arbor *B-C* supported at each end by the frame of the watch. The patent text limits itself to a bare description of the arbor. In the light of what we have seen of the shortcomings of the original model, however, the patent drawings tell that much more had been accomplished on the general design of a more workable rotary watch.

A square on arbor *C* at the back of the watch permits winding the main spring, which attaches to the largest diameter of *C*, a ratchet or winding click being supplied just under support *F*. The inner or front part *B* of the composite arbor projects from the front of the movement and revolves at the speed of the barrel arbor, which speed is not specified. Also, looking at the perspective view, we see that while the chronometer escapement has been retained, the balance has been placed eccentrically to make room for the center arbor. The balance now describes an orbit around the center of revolution. No driving train is shown, it being irrelevant to the patent, but there seems to be ample room for two intermediate wheels and their pinions between the escape wheel and the train cock boss, seen at the upper right in the perspective view of **Figure 4**. Adding one more wheel and pinion to the train would have the effect of reducing the number of revolutions required of the spring barrel. We have seen from examination of the patent model of the Hopkins rotary that this was necessary not only to reduce the number of turns of the main spring and barrel, but also to reduce the force transmitted to the escapement. There seems little reason from the foregoing observations and considerations to doubt that these modifications had been realized by the time of this patent. Again, no dial gearing is shown. If the need for special gearing existed at this time, it seems strange that it was not covered by patent as was done in the later patent **[endnote 10]** assigned to William B. Fowle. The only way to avoid special gearing would be to revolve the barrel and train each hour so that the minute hand could travel with them as it travels with the center wheel in conventional watches. Once this condition was set up, the usual dial gearing would apply.

Companion patent 165830 **(see Figure 5)** covers a mechanism to prevent overbanking of the balance wheel, primarily of a chronometer escapement. This, of course, was aimed at making it possible to use the escapement in connection with a mainspring of greatly varying power. We have seen that this condition of uneven power existed in the first Hopkins watch. While the condition was greatly improved in the second model (seen in **Figure 4**), it was surely present to some extent, as it is associated with every spring.

Overbanking protection may well have continued to be necessary, particularly if the gear ratio between escapement and barrel was low enough to permit hourly rotation of the barrel. The features covered by this patent were originally submitted as part of what later became patent 165831. Examination of the original manuscript patent file **[endnote 11]** shows that the patent application was separated into two on the suggestion of the patent examiner, who pointed out that two distinct and separate mechanisms were involved, either of which could be used without the other.

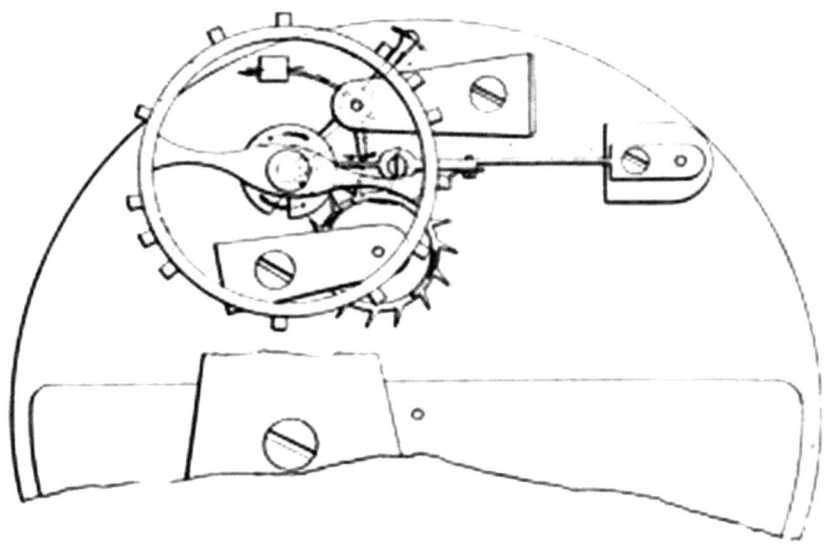

Figure 6 – rawing from U. S. Patent 179019 showing Hopkins' device to prevent the tripping of a chronometer escapement.

These two patents, which actually started out as one, appear to represent the watch as it was when Hopkins went to Waterbury, Connecticut, where he again met Edward A. Locke. They submitted this improved watch model to the Benedict and Burnham Manufacturing Co., which advised not manufacturing it until it was further developed. Hopkins went with his watch from there to Boston, where he conferred with George Merritt who, like Locke, was interested in getting into the manufacture of a low-priced watch. Merritt may have been the senior member of the Locke-Merritt team, or may simply have had more faith than his associates in Hopkins and his watch.

At any rate, he advanced expense money while further efforts at improvement were made **[endnote 12]** Hopkins' absence from the *Washington city directory* of 1877 is perhaps explained by this work he was doing on his patent. While this was completed to Hopkins' satisfaction, it still fell short of Merritt's idea of practicality, and the latter abandoned the idea of manufacturing the watch **[endnote 13]** what had started out as a very simple watch of few parts grew, with every effort to make it workable, more and more complicated by involved and expensive detail. It appears that Hopkins did not possess the rare gift of improvement by simplification. This is a rare gift, and one seldom possessed by an individual very closely and intensely involved in the minute details of a given problem.

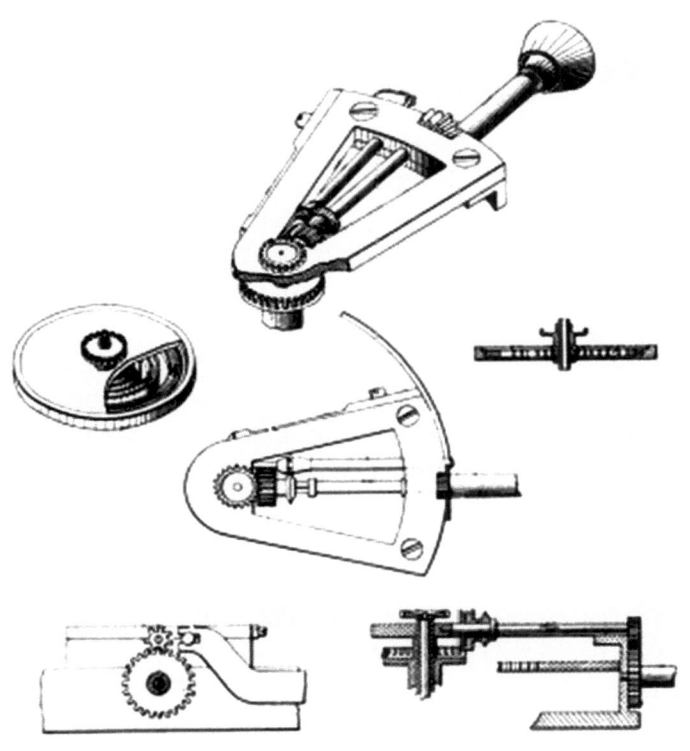

Figure 7 – Part of the Drawings from U. S. Patent 186838, showing the winding and setting mechanism very nearly as it was applied in the Auburndale rotary.

How long this period of development and experimentation required is unreported. It could hardly have started before early June of 1875, when application was made for the patent (165830) to prevent overbanking.

The cash book of William B. Fowle of Auburndale, Massachusetts, **[endnote 14]** tells us that he bought half of William D. Colt's half-interest in the Hopkins rotary in March 1876, partly for cash but including a royalty on each watch made. Half this royalty was to go to Hopkins, a quarter to William D. Colt, and a quarter to William B. Fowle.

Does patent 179019, issued June 20, 1876, to Hopkins, who assigned it on June 10, 1876, to Fowle, **[endnote 15]** represent the last improvement offered to Merritt? It covers a device actuated by a spur on a balance staff to lock the detent against tripping when in one position and to permit normal operation of the chronometer escapement when in the other position (see **Figure 6**).

Another patent applied for on January 12, 1876, was in prospect and finally issued as no. 186838 on January 30, 1877, assigned to William B. Fowle on November 21, 1876 **[endnote 16]**. This is much the most practical and useful patent in the series. A comparison of these (see **Figures 7** and **8**] with the Auburndale rotary watch (see **Figure 9**] shows a remarkable similarity between the inventor's conception and the product eventually manufactured. A practical center arbor to support and guide the entire rotating mechanism is here combined with a stem-winding and lever-setting mechanism and dial gearing in a well-thought-out arrangement.

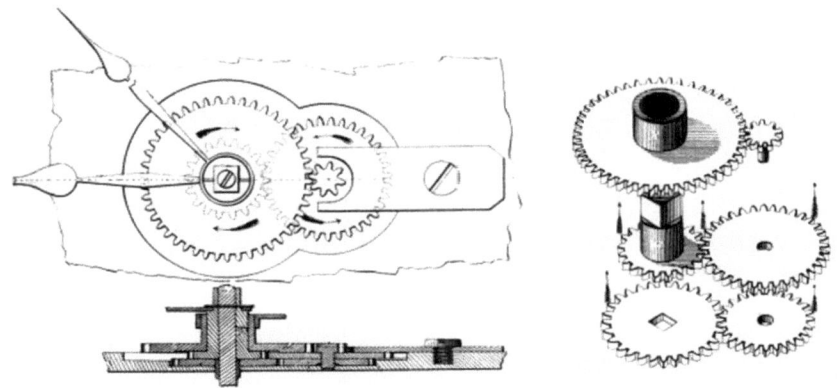

Figure 8 – Remaining Drawings from U. S. Patent 186838, showing the dial gearing used in the Auburndale rotary.

Here, where the story of the Hopkins watch diverges from the interests who later brought out the rival Waterbury watch, it seems appropriate to call the reader's attention to the basic points of novelty and merit in the Hopkins watch which carried over to what became the Waterbury, somewhat as a hereditary characteristic passes from generation to generation.

Previous writers have realized that one of these watches led to the other and have grouped them together because of the rotating feature which they shared in common. Beyond this point, they have treated the watches as though they had nothing in common. Actually several basic features of the Hopkins watch existed in both: the long narrow spring in a barrel approximately filling one side of the watch case, a train rotating in the center of the watch and driven by a planetary pinion in mesh with a gear fixed to the stationary part of the watch, a slow beat

21

escapement, and probably the hourly rotation of the train and escapement. When these details appeared in the first watches manufactured for Messrs Locke and Merritt by the Benedict and Burnham Manufacturing Co. and later the Waterbury Watch Co., they were vastly changed in detail and much better adapted to mass production, although still basically the same.

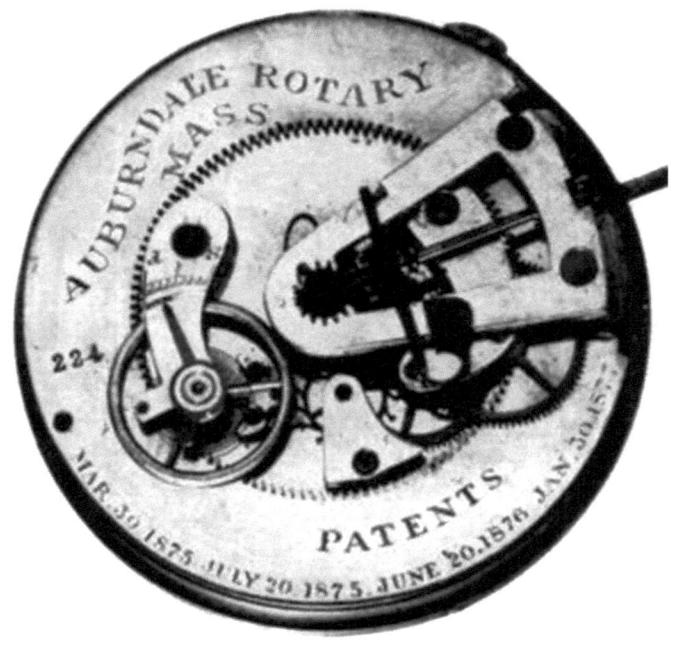

Figure 9 – Auburndale Rotary Watch Movement. (In the author's collection.)

The story of Hopkins' rotary watch now enters an entirely new setting with new financial backing which, however, had no apparent experience or background in mechanical work, much less watch manufacturing. Those with watchmaking experience who were brought into this new organization unquestionably did their best, based on past experience confined to conventional watches of much higher grade. Judging from the products turned out, however, they had great difficulty in making a clean break with their past and in producing a satisfactory low-priced watch of a new and radical concept. The market for watches, which had been depressed, was at this time reviving a little. The *Newton Journal* [endnote 17], referring to the American Watch Co. at Waltham reported: 'The hands employed in the caseroom and the machinists have been called in. All the works are to be started the first of September.'

Figure 10 – William B. Fowle, sponsor of the Auburndale Watch Co., after an engraving in S. F. Smith, *History of Newton, Massachusetts* (Boston, 1880).

THE NEW SPONSOR

William Bentley Fowle **(Figure 10)**, new partner with Hopkins and Colt in the watch, was born in Boston, Massachusetts on July 27, 1826. His father, William B. Fowle, Senior, a well-known Boston teacher and educator, had variously been a bookseller and conductor of a 'Female Monitorial School' **[endnote 18]**. The junior William B. Fowle we have first located as a ticket master with the Boston and Worcester Railroad in 1848 **[endnote 19]**, and he retained this listing in the directory through 1851. Starting in 1852 and continuing through 1862, with no indication of employer or occupation, he had an office at 9 Merchants Exchange.

In 1860 and 1862 he was a member of the Boston Common Council, and was president of that body in 1865. In 1862, after the second battle of Bull Run, he raised an infantry company for the 43rd Massachusetts Volunteers and was mustered in, September 24, 1862, with the rank of captain. From December 7, 1862, to March 4, 1863, he was commandant of the military post at Beaufort, North Carolina. He then reported to his regiment. On June 24, 1863, he was left sick at New Bern, North Carolina, by his company bound for Fortress Monroe. On July 21 he rejoined his company at Boston, Massachusetts, in time to be mustered out on July 30 at the expiration of his nine months' enlistment **[endnote 20]**.

Figure 11 – The Two Lever Escapements Used in the Auburndale Rotary. Note, in addition to the escapement, the absence of banking pins and the metal balance jewel in the escapement at the left, which is from watch No. 176. (Both watches in the author's collection.)

In the 1864 *Boston directory* we find him listed as treasurer of the Bear Valley Coal Co., and the North Mountain Coal Co., with an office at 38 City Exchange. This association with the coal business continued with changes unimportant to our story through the directories until 1877, in which year the name is dropped from the *Boston directory*, not to reappear until the directory of 1880, where he is listed at 'Herald Building, watches and timers.' This was apparently the sales office. The *Newton directory* of 1877 drops its previous listing of coal after Mr. Fowle's name and first mentions the Auburndale Watch Co. **[endnote 21]**. In 1866 Mr. Fowle established his home, Tanglewood, in Auburndale, a village in Newton not far from his boyhood home at West Newton and on the bank of the Charles River about two miles upstream from the

Waltham Watch Co. He served the town of Newton as selectman from 1869 through 1871, was an alderman in 1877, and mayor in 1878 and 1879 [endnote 22].

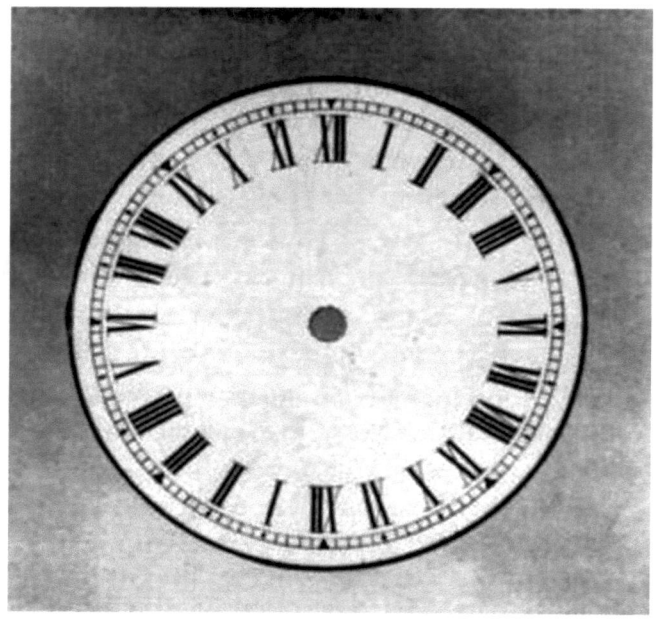

Figure 12 – A 24-Hour Dial for the rotary watch. (In the author's collection.)

William Atherton Wales of New York is credited with introducing Mr. Fowle to the Hopkins watch. No clue has come to light on what connection there was between Hopkins and Wales, who had been a partner in the large watch-importing house of Giles, Wales and Co., in New York and later a large stockholder in the United States Watch Co. of Marion, New Jersey, which had only ceased operation in 1874.

A patent **[endnote 23]** had been issued to Fayette S. Giles of New York, the leading figure in the United States Watch Co., for an improvement in stem-winding watches. This had presumably been available to his company.

In this winding mechanism a crown pinion driven by a clutch on the stem engages with a large ring gear, having 110 internal teeth, which in turn drives a gear on the barrel arbor.

The author has seen no watch, except the patent model **[endnote 24]**, containing this device, but the pillar plate of many of the United States Watch Co. movements were cut out, apparently to receive this ring gear.

The expense of cutting so many internal teeth in steel seems reason enough to explain why this patent did not become the basis for all their stem-wound models. Steel is far more difficult to cut than brass, resulting in a much greater consumption of time and cutters, both of which represent money to the manufacturer.

In the patent model, these ring-gear teeth have been cut by a milling cutter which did not pass through the ring and across the face of the teeth. This produced a gear somewhat resembling an internal bevel gear, one which could have only the merest contact with its mating pinion.

To make a durable gear for this application, it would be necessary to pass the cutter through the ring in line with the gear axis. This would require a special or, at least, radically modified gear-cutting machine with a cutter arbor shorter than the inside diameter of the gear. Into this short space the spindle bearings and means of driving the spindle would have to be crowded, along with the cutter.

Hopkins faced a problem similar to this in cutting the ring gear for his watch, except that the brass gear needed for the rotary watch could be cut far more easily and quickly. This may be the link which brought Wales and the defunct United States Watch Co. into the Auburndale picture. Another plausible link between Fowle and Wales involves a patent **[endnote 25]** Wales received for a pulley.

This, the now familiar device of interlocking conical sections so commonly used in variable speed V-belt drives, was assigned to G. E. Lincoln of Boston, Massachusetts.

George E. Lincoln was treasurer of the Mammoth Vein Consolidated Coal Co. at Boston in 1865, with an office adjoining that of Fowle. In addition, he boarded for many years at Auburndale **[endnote 26]** and he apparently owned the buildings about to be converted into a watch factory.

Thus, we see that Lincoln may very well have been the one who brought Fowle and Wales together.

Figure 13 – The Auburndale Timer with top plate, balance, and control mechanism removed to show the train. The conventional barrel has 66 teeth that drive a pinion on the so-called 10-minute staff. This staff carries on the dial end the pointer, which revolves in 10 minutes, as indicated on the dial. Also on this staff is an unspoked wheel of 80 driving the center, or minute, staff through a pinion of 8. In addition to the sweep hand (or hands in the case of the split model) indicating seconds up to a duration of one minute, there is a wheel of 80 driving a pinion of 8 on an intermediate staff. A wheel of 60 on this staff drives a pinion of 10 on the escape-wheel staff. A pointer on this last staff also carries the hand that indicates fractions of a second. (In the author's collection.)

William B. Fowle's cash book shows, on July 14, 1876, payment to Geo. E. Lincoln 'For large building used $200' and 'For small building used $30.' On July 21 is an entry 'Milo Lucas bal. of Building Contract $1605.25.' These with an entry on the preceding June 30, 'Milo Lucas on a/c Contract for Building' seem, with a July 25 entry 'W. E. C. Fowler, Painting Factory $64.91,' to cover the expense for the bare factory. The buildings, two stories high and measuring 40 x 20 and 32 x 20 feet, respectively, were located on the Weston bank of the Charles River, opposite Fowle's home, from which they could be reached by a private ferry. This pleasant bucolic location was not far upstream from that originally sought by the Boston Watch Co. when that firm was looking for a spot to move to from Roxbury in 1854. The situation of the factory was described as a wild and secluded glen **[endnote 27]**.

Another account **[endnote 28]** says:

The well appointed little steamer *White Swan*, owned and commanded by a Captain Gibbs, veteran of the last war, now plies regularly between Waltham and Auburndale Bridge, carrying picnic parties, etc.... Along the banks of the river are located the summer residences of Messrs. Cutter and Merrill, the elegant residence of R. M. Pulsifer, Mayor of Newton, the splendid mansion of Ex-Mayor Fowle, the Benyon mansion and others.... At sunset the river is alive with canoes, row-boats, shells and sailboats filled with ladies and gentlemen, adding with the delightful music, greatly to the natural charm of the scenery.

Figure 14 – Escape Wheel and Pallets of an Auburndale timer. With four pins in the escape wheel, this particular one beats eighths of a second. (In author's collection.)

This idyllic pastoral setting surely must have been a joy to all connected with the little watch factory. It seems to typify the atmosphere of wealth and leisure into which the infant industry was brought without adequate study of the problems it would be called upon to surmount.

The Auburndale machinery came from the United States Watch Co. factory at Marion, New Jersey, which, as we have seen, was closed in 1874. William A. Wales, who was associated with Fowle in the Auburndale 'adventure', had been secretary, treasurer, and director of this company. Most of the machinery came from George E. Hart and Co., of Newark, which had taken over much of the Company's equipment, eventually selling it to other factories. Warren E. Ray, a neighbor of Mr. Fowle's, commenced as manager of the factory in July 1876, and died suddenly of heart disease about October 1 of that year. He was soon succeeded by Mr. James H. Gerry, who had gone from Waltham to Newark in 1863 to superintend the building of the original machines for the United States factory.

The employees were chiefly drawn from other factories, principally the neighboring American Watch Co. at Waltham, and the defunct United States Watch Co., while some who needed no specific watchmaking skills perhaps never had worked in a watch factory before. Names, not already mentioned, that have been preserved are: George H. Bourne, L. C. Brown, Abraham Craig, Frederick H. Eaves, Henry B. Fowle, Benjamin F. Gerry, William H. Guest, Jose Guinan, Sadie Hewes, Isaac Kilduff (the watchman), Justin Hinds, E. Moebus, James O'Connell (the stationary engineer), Edwin H. Perry, Frank N. Robbins, John Rose, Thomas W. Shephard, William H. A. Simmons, Alfred Simpson, Thomas Steele, Oscar L. Strout, and George Wood. These, compiled from several sources **[endnote 29]**, represent only a few of the men who contributed their knowledge and skill to the enterprise; they are listed in alphabetical order because it has been found impossible to arrange them accurately according to position, magnitude of contribution, or length of service.

Of the five Hopkins patents **[endnote 30]** the first and the last are the ones covering the essential elements used in the Auburndale product.

The two patents assigned in half to William D. Colt apparently were never used, nor does the device shown in **Figure 6** seem to have been used, although these unused patents are listed on the Auburndale movements.

Now that the watch was in the hands of men accustomed to making watches, some modifications dictated by their experience and by considerations of expediency in manufacture were made. The movement that issued was 18 size, rather thick, cased at the factory in a nickel case made by the Thiery Watch Case Co. of Boston, Massachusetts. In the winding and setting mechanisms, some changes in details were made with respect to those shown in **Figure 7**.

The dial is mounted by means of a rim which snaps over the edge of the movement, as on a high-grade Swiss watch of the same era. The usual dial feet, if used, would have interfered with the rotation of the movement. For the same reason, of course, there is no dial indicating seconds.

Figure 15 – Verge and Lever for an Auburndale timer. The one on the left beats eighths of a second; that on the right beats quarters. (In author's collection.)

Five jewels are found in most instances, two cap jewels and two hole jewels for the balance staff and a jeweled impulse pin. One of the faults of the movement is that the cap and hole jewels on the balance are not separable for cleaning. After the jewels were inserted, part of the setting was spun down over them, making the assembly permanent. A few movements with only one jewel are known, the cap and hole jewels being metal 'jewels' likewise set under a spun-over rim. Whether or not the impulse jewel found in these last-mentioned movements is original or a later intrusion remains undetermined. It is easy to conceive that the factory would see no more necessity for an impulse jewel than for other jewels.

The lever escapement is the only one known to have been used, but two varieties of this are found (see **Figure 11**). One is a standard club-tooth lever with banking pins, the other, much more interesting because unconventional, has pointed pallets and all the lift on the escape wheel, which has very short stubby teeth, very much like the wheel of a pin-pallet escapement. No banking pins are used, the banking taking place between the pallets and the wheel. An examination of a number of these watches, with serial numbers ranging from 46 to 507 [endnote 31], reveals no correlation between the serial number and the style of escapement, from which one may conclude that the pointed pallet escapement was originally used; later four balance jewels were added, and the escapement changed to the conventional club-tooth pattern. As complaints came in about the defective running of the watch, these changes were apparently substituted at the factory in customers' watches. The movements with the pointed-pallet escapement seldom show much wear; on the other hand, watch no. 224 [endnote 32], which has the conventional escapement and five jewels, is very much worn and must have run for many years.

These watches are stem wound by turning opposite to the usual direction and are set through the winding crown after actuating a setting lever located under the front bezel. The plates, bridges, and ring gear are nickel-plated and highly buffed, making a very showy movement, the only instances of such a finish on watches in the author's experience. In **Figure 12** is shown a 24-hour dial to fit the movement. Special dial gearing would be required for the hour hand to accompany this dial.

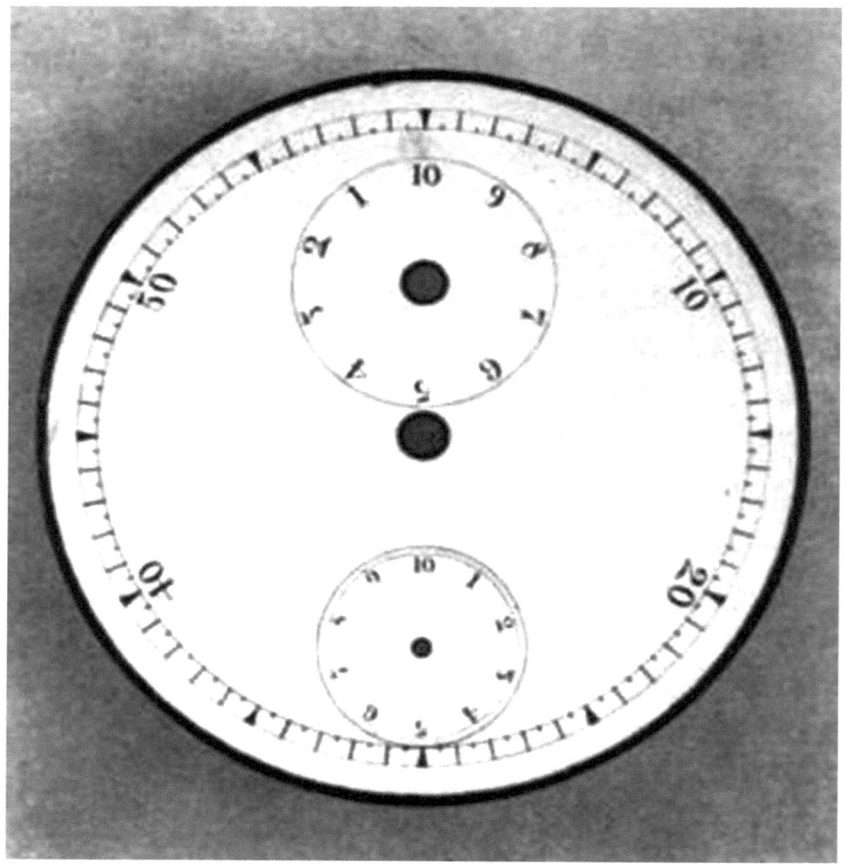

Figure 16 – Dial forb 1/10-Second Model Auburndale timer. (In author's collection.)

The first of these watches were placed on the market in 1877, priced at $10.00 to the trade. Soon complaints came in that they were defective in operation and many were returned. We have seen from the specimens examined that there seems to have been no established model produced in quantity. The dial and the number of jewels varied, as well as the escapement, suggesting that the owners were groping for a salable variant of the design for which they had tooled the factory. Probably the pointed pallet escapement was used first, it being the less expensive of the two. In addition to the saving effected by not requiring banking pins, the escape wheel was much cheaper to cut, as the teeth were very short and strong (see **Figure 11**). Since the banking took place between the pallets and the escape wheel, there was no adjustment for the amount of slide; and since the watches were not made to close tolerances, the slide was necessarily excessive and consequently power consuming. The conventional club-tooth escapement was probably substituted as less troublesome, although the banking pins were fixed and could only be adjusted by bending them. The pallets remained solid steel, without adjustable stone inserts.

At this stage of affairs approximately $140,000 had been invested in the venture, the market was already glutted with conventional watches which enjoyed the confidence of retailers, and the Auburndale Rotary had won a bad reputation. The success of any watch depends largely on the confidence the retail dealers have in it. They are looking for a product easy to sell at an attractive profit, as well as one that will stay sold and create a satisfied customer. Fowle was of course very much disappointed; before going into the venture he had been advised that he could expect to produce 200 watches per day on an expenditure of $16,000 **[endnote 33]**. The watches reached the market at a time, the fall of 1877, almost coincidental with the application by D. Azro A. Buck for patents on what was to become the Waterbury rotary. These patents represented a new and economically sound expression of the basic ideas of Hopkins. The Waterbury associates immediately commenced work aimed at getting their watch on the market by June 1878 **[endnote 34]**.

News of this certainly reached Auburndale where they were not only well aware of the cost of producing their rotary but were also aware of the strict cost and performance studies which Locke and Merritt would apply to any watch before they would invest in it. Knowledge of this very able and well organized rival, coupled with the troubles experienced in manufacturing and selling the Auburndale Rotary, seem to account for the decision to abandon it. It was unfortunate that the timing of events happened just as it did for a little more work on the Auburndale and the tools for making it would probably have placed it on a firm footing in the trade, although obviously it could never compete with what eventually became the low-priced watch, really a scaled-down alarm clock minus the alarm mechanism.

It is said that about one thousand of the 'Rotaries' were made. The highest serial number to come to the author's attention, 507, may indicate that only a part of the watches started were finished.

Accounts agree **[endnote 35]** that the next product of the factory was a 'Timer' containing a novel escapement patented on May 28, 1878 **[endnote 36]** by William A. Wales. Early specimens are marked 'Pat. Applied For,' but one with the serial number 996 **[endnote 37]** bears no reference at all to a patent, presumably because issuance of the patent or patents was imminent. Apparently, the timer was in full production before the patent was issued on May 28. Specimens with higher serial numbers are stamped with three patent dates, May 28, 1878 **[endnote 38]**, June 24, 1879, and September 30, 1879, as seen in **Figure 13**, which also shows the arrangement of the train. In this escapement the escape wheel **(Figure 14)** carries in the rim any suitable number of steel pins all on the same radius from, and parallel to, the axis of wheel rotation. In all cases, the wheel makes one revolution per second. The verge **(Figures 14 and 15)** is so proportioned that the distance between the points of repose on the entrance and exit pallets will stop the wheel at intervals equal to half the angular distance between the pins.

In other words, with two pins in the escape wheel the escapement will beat quarters of a second, because starting from a point of repose the wheel will be arrested on the other point of repose after turning through 90°. With four pins in the escape wheel and a suitably proportioned verge, the escape wheel advances in steps of 45° and beats eighths of a second. The growing trend in this period to standardize the timing of sporting events in intervals of fifths of a second is reflected in still another model having five pins in the escape wheel and beating tenths of a second. By the nature of the verge in this escapement, it will be seen that the number of beats must be twice the number of pins in the escape wheel, leaving no way to secure an odd number of beats per second, hence the 1/10-second model. This must have been a less desirable form because of the much smaller verge required, plus the problem of accelerating so much mass from a dead stop 600 times per minute.

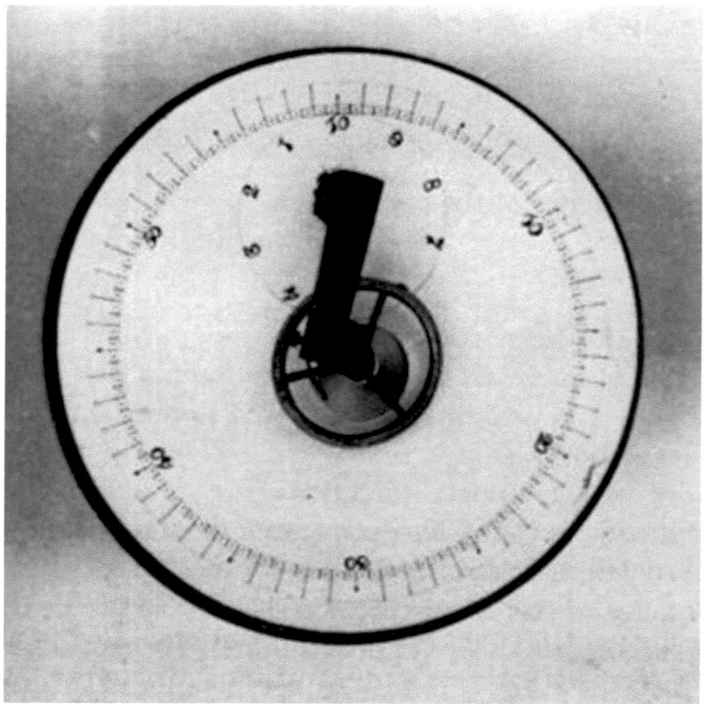

Figure 17 – A Timer Dial that is probably either experimental or very early. Note that the fractions of a second (quarters) are shown on the outside dial instead of on a separate dial. This dial was converted at the factory for use as the base of a hairspring vibrating stand. A dial different from this but having the same arrangement of circles is known. (In author's collection.)

Figure 16 illustrates a dial for this 1/10-second model which the author found in a lot of unused parts left over when the factory closed. The watch had an 18-size $^3/_4$-plate movement with grained nickel finish. The escapement is special, as we have seen, but the fork, roller, and balance action are conventional. There are five jewels, four to support the balance staff and an impulse jewel. The barrel arbor comes through the top plate with a square, as in a keywind watch, but is fitted with a winding handle, so that a key is unnecessary. This handle appears to be an afterthought, because on the earlier models (those with serial numbers below 1,000), the barrel arbor is short, barely long enough to attach the winding handle; later this arbor was made longer. Patent 204274 issued to Benjamin Wormelle of Brighton, Massachusetts, on May 28, 1878, the same date as Wales' escapement patent, may have suggested this winding handle. On watches with higher serial numbers, there are two arrows on the handle to show the direction to wind.

The earliest of these timers had a slide on the side of the case to stop the movement by means of a piece of thin spring steel applied roughly tangentially to the smooth rim of the three-arm, solid steel balance wheel. When this action is reversed to start the movement, the spring, in retracting from the wheel rim, starts the wheel swinging. Soon this slide on the case was dispensed with by fitting a curved sheet-metal rack into a groove turned in the edge of the balance cock. Engaging this rack was a pinion with a square hole through which the square stem could slide to set the hands back to zero as it had from the beginning, while turning the stem now would actuate the pinion and rack to start and stop the movement, as the slide in the case had originally done.

Various minor changes, dictated by experience and the need for economy in manufacture, were made in these movements. After about the first thousand, the diameter of the balance was reduced from approximately .700 to about .530 inch. This smaller wheel was, of course, much more suitable to vibrate at the faster speeds required on the models beating eighths and tenths of a second. At some time between the manufacture of watches bearing serial numbers 3135 and 3622, the formerly separate winding pawl and spring were combined into one piece that could be entirely made in a punch press. Another economy move was to stamp the name and patents in place of hand engraving. For a long time hand engraving was used, although stamping had been used from the beginning on the earlier rotary watch.

The case was very similar to that used on the rotary. The dial, of white enamel with snap rim fastened by a screw **[endnote 39]**, carried three graduated circles, an outer circle graduated in seconds up to sixty surrounding two smaller subsidiary dials. The top one of these smaller dials recorded minutes elapsed up to ten and the lower one recorded fractions of a second. The same dial was used on movements indicating quarters and eighths of seconds, all being graduated in eighths. A dial without provision for indicating the fractions of a second on a separate small dial may be seen in **Figure 17**.

This last has been made into a stand for hair spring work and is shown with balance and spring just as it came from the Auburndale factory with balance spring and wheel for a timer still in place.

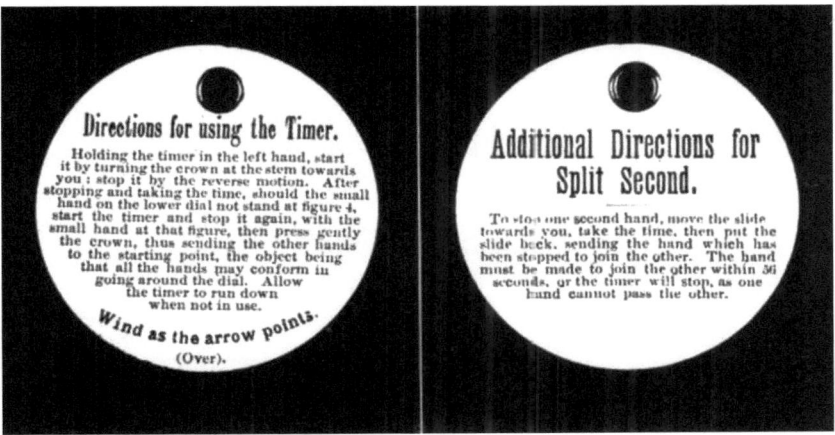

Figure 18 – Tag Displaying Directions for Use of the Auburndale Timer. (In author's collection.)

Left: Directions for using the Timer. Holding the timer in the left hand, start by turning the crown at the stem towards you: stop it by the reverse motion. After stopping and taking the time, should the small hand on the lower dial not stand at **Figure 4**, start the timer and start it again, then press gently the crown, thus sending the other hands to the starting point, the object being that all the hand may conform in going around the dial. Allow the timer to run down when not in use. Wind as the arrow points (Over).

Right: Additional directions for split second. To stop one second hand, move the slide towards you, take the time, then put the slide back, sending the hand which has been stopped to join the other. The hand must be made to join the other within 36 seconds, or the timer will stop, as one hand cannot pass the other.

43

The sweep second hand and the minute register hand are attached to heart-shaped cams friction driven from their respective staffs. They are reset by a bar pivoted beneath the dial and actuated by the stem through pressure on the crown. An original instruction tag as sent from the factory with these timers is seen in **Figure 18**.

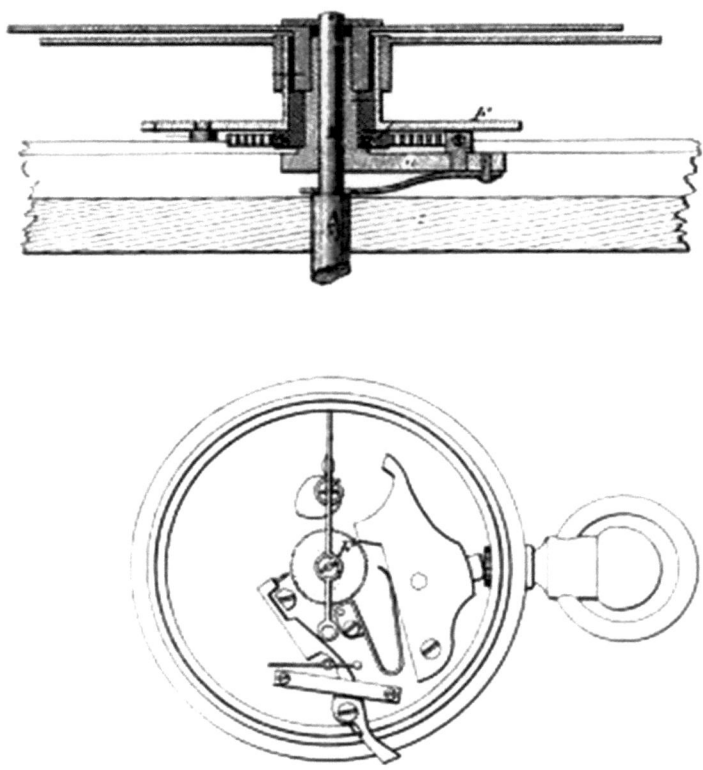

Figure 19 – Split Second Mechanism of the Auburndale timer, as shown in drawings from U. S. patent 220195, issued September 30, 1879.

Figure 19 shows the mechanism of the split-second model as represented in U. S. patent 220195 of September 30, 1879, issued to William A. Wales and assigned to William B. Fowle **[endnote 40]**.

A split-second mechanism is used to time the finish of two horses in the same race or any other similar event. In usual watches of this nature the watch will run along indefinitely with the extra or split second hand stopped, although this hand will not record more than a difference of one minute from the main sweep hand.

This was not true of the Auburndale, as pointed out in the instructions. The reason for this is that motion is conveyed to this hand through a hair spring, which would be damaged if allowed to overwind. To prevent this, a stop is interposed which will halt the entire watch unless directions are followed.

The serrated wheel *F*, of hardened steel, driving the second sweep hand, is cut on the edge with 120 serrations; stopping of this hand therefore is only to the nearest half second, regardless of how minutely the escapement is dividing time.

This is rather a serious defect as, if timing a horse race as an example, the time of the fastest horse is taken on this hand which registers a lesser degree of accuracy than the time recorded on the second and less important horse. A general view of one of these watches is seen in **Figure 20**.

Figure 20 – Auburndale Timer With Split Second Hand. Note the stop and start lever for the 'split' hand at the side of the case. (In author's collection.)

SUCCESS AND FAILURE

It would be pleasant to report that after the fiasco of the rotary model, these timers were a financial success, but the facts indicate otherwise. They were well-built and reliable, so that the trade was pleased to stock and promote them. The public responded well when in the market for a timer, as might be expected, since no other stop watch with fractional second dial or split-second hand was made in the country. Those imported from abroad were many times as expensive. Unfortunately, the demand was seasonal. Sometimes, during the racing season, demand would reach 400 per month, while at other seasons of the year practically none at all were sold. Some remained in stock during the remaining life of the company, as is shown by the following advertisement **[endnote 41]** which was accompanied by an illustration of the watch:

The old reliable Auburndale Chronograph Timers, for sale by Edward H. Brown, No. 16 Maiden Lane, New York. The manufacture of these watches having been discontinued for reasons entirely apart from their value and reliability, the stock in existence is very limited, and is now in the hands of Mr. Edward H. Brown, No. 16 Maiden Lane, New York City, the well known and reliable dealer in Watches, Diamonds and Jewelry. The Auburndale timer has been in the hands of a number of competent judges, and has always been found to be accurate. It is of convenient size, and is contained in a German silver case, nickel plated. The timers are manufactured in two qualities, without split seconds for $15 and with the split second for $25. They all have minute, second and lightning hands. We recommend all desiring a cheap and reliable timer to apply at once to Mr. Brown, No. 16 Maiden Lane, New York.

A steadier market was sought with the introduction of a low-priced 3/4-plate, back-setting, 18-size watch to compete, it was hoped, with the full-plate watches of similar price made by the established companies. Nearly all these watches had seven jewels, some few had more. The majority were key wind and set with a folding winding key permanently attached to the barrel arbor, as in **Figure 21**. These were named 'Lincoln' for Mr. Fowle's son, Lincoln A. Fowle **[endnote 42]** and had a solid steel balance with screws and the general appearance of a compensated balance.

Figure 21 – Auburndale Three-Quarter Plate Watch, typical of both Lincoln and Bentley grades. (In author's collection.)

A stem-wound, lever-set edition of the same basic watch was named 'Bentley' for Bentley D. Fowle, another son **[endnote 43]**. This had a cut bimetallic balance and higher finish. Conventional gilt finish was used on both of these models, although one isolated specimen found in factory remainders **[endnote 44]** has a bright nickel finish comparable with the rotary watch. These watches were designed by Chauncey Hartwell **[endnote 45]** after J. H. Gerry had removed to Lancaster, where the Lancaster Watch Co., organized in August 1877, was attempting to bring a line of watches onto the market although beset by acute financial woes similar to those building up at Auburndale. To return to our 3/4-plate watches, it may be said that they were well-made for the price, reliable, and successful from a manufacturing point of view, but could not be sold at a figure high enough to return a profit on the manufacture.

Up to this time, about November 1, 1879, the Auburndale Watch Co., had existed as a private company; now it was incorporated with a book value of $500,000, and William B. Fowle, who at this point had invested about $250,000 (mostly unrecoverable) in the enterprise, was elected president, and George H. Bourne was elected secretary and treasurer. After a quantity of these Lincoln and Bentley watches had been manufactured [endnote 46] and it had become clear that they could not be attractively priced to the trade, the company sought a product adapted to their factory equipment for which a constant market could be found. The product chosen was a line of metallic thermometers **[endnote 47]**. Two patents, 240058 and 240059, were issued to William A. Wales, assignor to the Auburndale Watch Co., of Weston, Massachusetts, on April 12, 1881. Whether these patents represent the first thermometers made at Auburndale or reflect the result of experience gained in making conventional models is not clear. The earliest evidence dating the appearance of the thermometer is the 1881 *Boston Directory* which appeared on July 1. This illustrates the same model of thermometer seen in **Figure 22**. The patents cover means of eliminating springs of any sort from the mechanism, so that the hand or dial pointer is entirely under the influence of the fused bimetallic thermal strips. Manufacture of the timers was carried along with thermometer manufacture at first, but production of the timer was finally dropped, as the stock on hand was constantly increasing, and for a while the factory was at last operated at a profit, on thermometers alone. These were furnished in cases from 20 inches in diameter down to the size of a ten cent piece, according to the advertising.

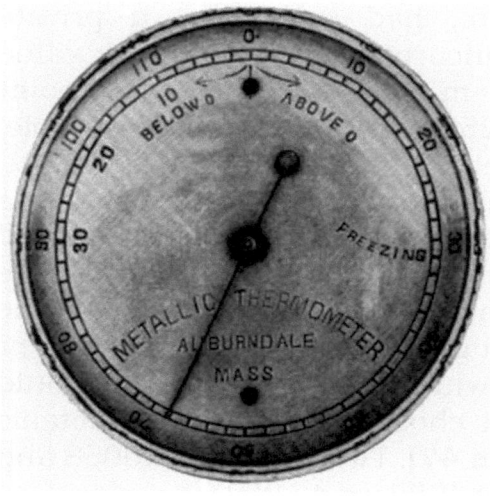

Figure 22 – Auburndale Thermometer, about 1 3/4 inches in diameter. (In author's collection.)

Unfortunately, Mr. Fowle had suffered so much loss through the watch venture and from other investments that he was forced to make an assignment of his personal estate. The watch company, without his support, was carrying too large a burden of debt to be self-supporting. In the fall of 1883 a voluntary assignment was made, and the equipment was sold in February 1884 **[endnote 48]**.

The *Newton directory* of 1885 lists W. B. Fowle as a thermometer manufacturer on Woodbine Street, 'house near.' His home, 'Tanglewood,' was on Woodbine Street and perhaps the thermometer business was operating in one of the outbuildings. William A. Wales assigned to the Auburndale Watch Co. patent 276101, of December 4, 1883, covering details of a unit counter for keeping score in games, and for similar work. Among the relics in the author's collection is a box bearing the label 'Auburndale Counter, W. B. Fowle & Son, Auburndale, Mass.' These counters were packed two in a box, the box just mentioned being suitable to contain counters the size of the thermometer in **Figure 22**.

Figure 23 shows a larger counter measuring 4 1/2 inches in diameter. From this and the fact that Fowle as late as 1887, is carried in the *Newton directory* as a manufacturer of metallic thermometers, it seems that some attempt was made after the dissolution of the watch company to carry on manufacturing, or perhaps only the assembly on a small scale of parts previously manufactured. The *Directory* of 1889 lists Fowle as an accountant on Ash Street, Auburndale. He had bought this property in

1887, presumably after disposing of 'Tanglewood' which now would be too large for his needs. In the editions of 1891 and 1893 he is listed as United States collector of internal revenue, with an office at the Post Office building, Boston. In 1895, he appears as an accountant at the same address, and from then to his death in 1902 he is listed as an accountant at his home address in Auburndale.

Figure 23 – Auburndale Counter. Pressure on the projecting stem indexes the inner dial, showing through the window, at the same time ringing a bell. This dial is numbered from zero through six. The outside hand is held in place by friction and is manually set as desired. There is no connection with the inner mechanism.

Jason R. Hopkins, inventor of the first Auburndale product, passed away in Washington late the same year, 1902, having spent all the intervening years as a watchmaker.

THE LESSON

The life of a pioneer has always been arduous. The story we have just reviewed illustrates this. Hopkins was a successful workman with clever and novel ideas. Fowle had been very successful in an entirely unrelated field. Wales had been very successful in importing and selling watches, but the watch factory which he had owned in part had failed, the fault more probably that of the times than of the man. The various superintendents and foremen were first-class men with ample background in making conventional watches. At the time, no one could have had experience in manufacturing exactly the grade and type of watch being attempted, for this was the pioneer effort.

The country was in the grip of a long, lingering depression following the Civil War. Money was tight. The Auburndale Rotary was conceived as a very low-priced watch which would at the same time include the desirable and unusual feature of close timekeeping. Could these ideals have been adhered to, there is little reason to question that it would have found a market, even in hard times.

We have seen that every effort to improve the original watch added to its cost, and here lies the real reason why it failed to win acceptance. By the time it reached the market it was no longer priced below conventional watches and at least some specimens were not reliable in performance. To make matters even worse, the best features of Hopkins' rotary watch had been incorporated by Locke and Merritt into a competing rotary watch much better engineered for cheap mass production.

At this point, the only hope for the factory seemed to be the manufacture of some other watch or similar small mechanism. The Auburndale timer, with the exception perhaps of the split-second model, was a triumph mechanically, and it returned a profit, but not enough to meet the financial needs of its sponsors. Much the same may be said of all the later Auburndale products.

The rotary had been of doubtful value when Flowe bought it, and the new organization was not able to contribute the necessary manufacturing engineering to make it a successful product. By the time this necessity was recognized, debts had mounted to the point where later products, which might have been successful on their own, were not able to carry the burden. The whole affair can be viewed as a very expensive educational adventure, from which the students were not able to salvage enough to put their education to any use.

Surely they received a clear illustration of how dangerous it can be to engage in an enterprise without sufficient background or a long and careful study of design, manufacturing processes, costs, and market and sales analysis. For although numerous fortunes have been made in watch manufacturing, many more have been lost, and often those who put every effort at their command into such ventures came away with only sad experience as their reward. Thus ended the story of the Auburndale Watch Company.

Endnotes:

[1] Paul M. Chamberlain, *It's about time*, New York, 1947, p. 362.

[2] British patent 21421, granted January 21, 1893.

[3] Chamberlain, *op. cit.* (footnote 1), pp. 229, 230.

[4] Cat. no. 309025; U. S. patent 161513, July 20, 1875.

[5] Those who have seen the Waterbury watch, which developed from this design, may be drawn to the conclusion that this explains why it took so long to wind the Waterbury. Such is not really the case; in the Waterbury the winding wheel (which is on the outer rim of the barrel) was nearly as large as the inside diameter of the case while the pinion engaging with it was of only nominal diameter. This meant that one turn of the winding crown wound the barrel a much smaller fraction of a revolution than in a watch of conventional design.

[6] District of Columbia death record 145,013.

[7] Hopkins is not in the *Washington and Georgetown directory* of 1860 or 1862, and 1861 was not available to check. Starting with 1863 he is listed each year through 1871. Starting with 1872 Boyd's *Directory of the District of Columbia* lists Hopkins as a resident each year (including 1902, the year of his death at 84 years) except 1877, when he was out of the city in connection with the exploitation of his rotary watch patents. Carl W. Drepperd, *American clocks and clockmakers* (Garden City, N.Y., 1947), in referring to Hopkins, says, 'Lincoln, Me. 1840's-1850's: Bangor, Me., to 1862. Inventor of the Auburndale Watch. Also manufactured pianos and clock cases.'

[8] Chas. S. Crossman, 'A complete history of watch and clock making in America,' *Jewelers Circular and Horological Review*, January 1888, pp. 400, 401. This history ran as a continuing series of short articles appearing over a period of years. In his sketch of the Waterbury Watch Co., Crossman gives the name as William D. Coates, a name not found in Boyd's *Directory of the District of Columbia* for 1875. The directory does, however, contain the name of William D. Colt, a patent attorney.

[9] U. S. patents 165830 and 165831, granted July 20, 1875.

[10] U. S. patent 186838, January 30, 1877.

[11] Patent file 165831, records of the Patent Office in the National Archives, Washington, D. C.

[12] Crossman, *op. cit.* (footnote 8), January 1888, p. 32.

[13] *Ibid.*, p. 33.

[14] William B. Fowle's 'Cash book', commenced January 1, 1873, and closed February 21, 1882, plus 'Cash Book #5 Leaves 1 to 20 inclusive. All that were used up to my failure on August 4, 1883,' are in the author's possession. They contain many entries on the 'Watch Adventure' and later 'Aub Watch Co.' mixed in with other entries referring to everything from killing pigs to extensive stock, bond, and real estate transactions.

[15] U. S. Patent Office digest of assignments, vol. H9V, p. 13, stored at Franconia, Virginia, Accession no. 57A393.

[16] *Ibid.*, p. 76.

[17] August 26, 1876, p. 2., under the heading of Waltham Items, 'Signs of a revival of business at the Watch Works in Waltham.'

[18] *Stimpson's Boston directory*, 1840.

[19] *Adams' new directory of the City of Boston*, 1847-48, 1849-50, 1851.

[20] Records of Veterans Administration, pension application 666 675, National Archives, Washington, D. C.

[21] The *Newton directory* at this time was issued biennially on odd numbered years.

[22] S. F. Smith, *History of Newton, Massachusetts*, Boston 1880, p. 833.

[23] U. S. patent 65208, issued May 28, 1867, all rights assigned to Giles, Wales and Co., March 4, 1867 and recorded March 8, 1867, at U. S. Patent Office, liber G9, p. 100.

[24] In the U. S. National Museum, cat. no. 309021.

[25] U. S. patent 179746, issued July 11, 1876.

[26] *Boston directory*, 1865 through 1872.

[27] M. F. Sweitser, *King's handbook of Newton, Massachusetts*, Boston, Mass., 1889, p. 203.

[28] Smith, *op. cit.* (footnote 22), p. 20.

[29] The sources used were Crossman, *op. cit.* (footnote 8), December 1887; Henry G. Abbot, *Watch factories of America*, Chicago, 1888, pp. 93-95; *Newton directory* for 1875, 1877, 1879, 1881, 1883, 1884-85, and 1885; *Waltham-Watertown directory* for 1877-78, 1880, 1882, 1884; and William B. Fowle, 'Cash book' (see footnote 14).

[30] U. S. patents 161513, applied for November 13, 1873, issued March 30, 1875; 165830, applied for July 14, 1875, issued July 20, 1875; 165831, applied for June 9, 1875, issued July 20, 1875; 179019, applied for May 25, 1876, issued June 20, 1876; and 186838, applied for January 12, 1876, issued January 30, 1877. A French patent was issued to Hopkins on September 12, 1876, and a Belgian patent on September 30, 1876. For lack of records neither has been positively identified but presumably they are for the same device covered in U. S. patent 179019.

[31] No. 46 courtesy of the late C. A. Ilbert (this watch is now in the Science Museum, South Kensington, London); 124, 176, 224, 241 in the author's collection; 161 Abbot, *op cit.* (footnote 29); 250 Henry Ford Museum, Dearborn, Michigan; 361 F. Earl Hackett; 387 Dr. Alfred G. Cossidente; 403 Dr. W. B. Stephens; 423 Crossman, *op cit.* (footnote 8); and an unnumbered movement illustrated in *American Jeweler*, December 1898, vol. 17, no. 12, p. 371.

[32] In the author's collection.

[33] Crossman, *op. cit.* (footnote 8), December 1887, p. 400.

[34] Crossman, *op. cit.* (footnote 8), January 1888, p. 33.

[35] Crossman, *op. cit.* (footnote 8), January 1888, pp. 400-401; Abbot, *op. cit.* (footnote 29).

[36] U. S. patent 204400.

[37] U. S. National Museum cat. no. 248691.

[38] U. S. patent 204400. The text of this patent speaks of dividing the second into 'halves, quarters, eighths, etc.' and in the summation of claims of 'an escape wheel, *A*, provided with one or more pairs of pins...' showing that measuring tenths of a second with a five-pin escape wheel was not conceived at this time. It is interesting to note that in referring to the drawings shown in figure 12 the text states 'In the present instance two pairs of pins are used to denote quarter seconds.' Only one pair of pins is shown, which is correct. This seems, however, to reflect carelessness on the part of patent attorneys and examiners, as the error exists in the original manuscript patent application preserved in the National Archives, Washington, D. C.

[39] U. S. patent 216917, issued to William A. Wales and assigned to William B. Fowle, was applied for on November 1, 1878, after the device was already in use on earlier specimens of these watches.

[40] The mechanism was also covered by British patent 3893, issued September 27, 1879, to Philip Syng Justice on behalf of William B. Fowle.

[41] *The Jewelers Circular and Horological Review*, July 1884.

[42] *Newton directory*, 1884-85; Crossman, *op. cit.* (footnote 8), December 1887.

[43] Records of Veterans Administration, pension application WE 666 675 of Mary E. Fowle (widow of William B. Fowle).

[44] Serial 926, in author's collection.

[45] *Newton directory*, 1879.

[46] Each model of watch made at Auburndale was numbered in its own series, starting at number 1, contrary to the usual watch factory practice where blocks of serial numbers are assigned to different models. Other Auburndale products seem not to have borne serial numbers.

[47] Crossman, *op. cit.* (footnote 8), December 1887.

[48] *Ibid.*

Notes:

Notes: